THIS BOOK BELONGS TO:

Made in the USA
Monee, IL
29 November 2021

83425833R00065